What's in this book

This book belongs to

_____

他们说什么语言？
What languages do they speak?

学习内容 Contents

沟通 Communication

说说某人的国籍
Talk about someone's nationality

说说某人会说的语言
Talk about the languages someone speaks

背景介绍：
来自不同国家和地区的小朋友说不同的语言。

生词 New words

★	中国	China
★	中国人	Chinese (people)
★	英国	the United Kingdom
★	英国人	British
★	美国	the United States
★	美国人	American
★	汉语	Chinese (language)
★	英语	English (language)
★	会	can, to be able to
★	说	to speak

汉语
你好

韩语
안녕하세요

阿拉伯语
مرحبا

Hello

英语
Hola

德语
Hallo

日语
こんにちは

法语
Bonjour

俄语
привет

西班牙语

葡萄牙语
Olá

写　　　　to write

国家　　　country

外来词
Loan words

句式 Sentence patterns

你是哪国人？
Which country are you from?

你会不会说英语？
Can you speak English?

我会说英语和汉语。
I can speak English and Chinese.

跨学科学习 Project

认识世界语言
Learn about world languages

参考答案：
1 Yes, I know some of them. This is English. This is ...
2 I speak English/Japanese/German.
3 I want to learn Chinese/Spanish/French.

Get ready

1 Do you know the languages in the picture?

2 What language do you speak?

3 What language do you want to learn?

故事大意：
不同国家和地区的小朋友除了会说自己国家的语言，还会说英语，大家都是好朋友。

zhōng guó
中国

zhōng guó rén
中国人

你好

shuō
说

hàn yǔ
汉语

汉语又称中文，是中国的官方语言。除中国外，汉语也使用于新加坡、马来西亚等东南亚国家和美国、加拿大等国的华人地区。汉语是全世界使用人数最多的语言。

我们是中国人，我们说汉语。

参考问题和答案：

1 Look at the map. Which country is it? (It is China.)

2 What nationality are the children? (They are Chinese.)

3 What language do they speak? (They speak Chinese.)

yīng guó rén

英国人

yīng guó

英国

yīng yǔ

英语

英语是英国、美国、加拿大、新西兰和澳大利亚等国家的官方语言，是全世界最广泛使用的语言。

Hello

我们是英国人，我们说英语。

参考问题和答案：

1 Look at the flag that the boy is holding. Which country's national flag is it? (It is the national flag of the UK.)

2 What nationality are the children? (They are British.)

3 What language do they speak? (They speak English.)

měi guó rén
美国人

měi guó
美国

Hello

我们是美国人，我们也说英语。

参考问题和答案：
1 Look at the map. Which country is it? (It is the United States.)
2 What nationality are the children? (They are American.)
3 What language do they speak? (They speak English.)

参考问题和答案：

1 Do you think the children are from the same country? (No, they are from different countries.)
2 They can speak the same language. Look at the word in the purple speech bubble. What language is it? (It is English.)

guó jiā
国家

"会"表示能够、熟习，
如"会唱歌"。

huì
会

Hello

我们是不同国家的人，
我们都会说英语。

xiě

写

参考问题和答案：

1 Do you think the children are good friends? (Yes, they are.)
2 The children are from different countries. Why can they become good friends? (Because they can use the same language to communicate.)

我们也会写一样的文字，
我们都是朋友。

1　Where are you from? (I am from Australia/France.)
2　Can you speak English or Chinese? (I can speak English./I can speak both of them.)

你是哪国人？你会不会
说英语？会不会说汉语？

Let's think

1 Match the countries to the flags. 提醒学生对照第4至6页的内容完成题目。

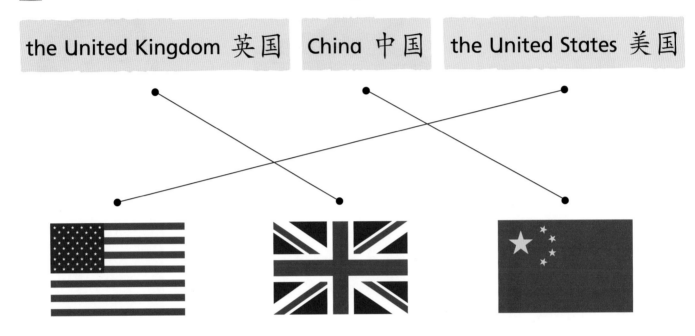

the United Kingdom 英国　China 中国　the United States 美国

2 Do you know where on the world map are China, the United Kingdom and the United States? Discuss with your friend what you know about these countries.

New words

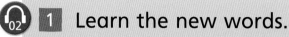

1 Learn the new words.

英语
English
会
说
汉语
写
国家

中国　中国人　　英国　英国人　　美国　美国人

2 What nationalities are they? What languages do they speak?
Write the letters. 提醒学生在方框内填a至c选项，在话框内填d或e选项。

a 中国人　b 英国人　c 美国人　d 英语　e 汉语

d

c

自由女神像（Statue of Liberty）
位于美国纽约。

e

a

长城（the Great Wall）
位于中国北方地区。

d

b

伊丽莎白塔（the Elizabeth
Tower），又称大本钟（Big
Ben），位于英国伦敦。

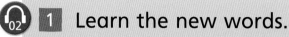

听听说说 Listen and say

第一题录音稿：
1 他是中国人。他会说汉语。
2 他们会说英语。
3 她是美国人。她会说英语，也会说汉语。

03 **1** Listen, number and say.

2

1

你好。

3

04 **2** Look at the pictures. Listen to the sto

① 你会不会说英语？

我会说英语。

③ 你是哪国人？

我是英国人。

nd say.

你是哪国人?

我是中国人。

你会不会写?

会说汉语，不会写。

告诉学生，询问他人是否能做某件事情可以使用"……会不会……？"或"……会……吗？"的句式。

3 Write the letters. Role-play with your friend.

a 汉语 b 会不会 c 哪 d 会

1

你是___c___国人?
你___d___说英语吗?
你喜欢看书吗?

我是英国人，我会说英语，我喜欢看书。

2

你是中国人吗?
你说___a___吗?
你___b___说英语?

我是中国人，我会说汉语和英语。

3

你是哪国人?
你喜欢做什么?
你___b___说汉语?

我是美国人，我喜欢唱歌，我不会说汉语。

Task

让学生课前上网搜索偶像的相关资料，再在课上三人一组讨论，最后每人用中文介绍一位人物。

Paste a photo of someone you admire in the space below. Introduce him/her to your friend.

他/她叫……

他/她是……人。

他/她……岁。

他/她会说……

和……

你认识他/她吗？

Paste your photo here.

提醒学生，"叫"字后边通常都跟名字。"是……人"中间通常是一个人家乡的国家或城市名称，表示这个人来自哪里。

Game

Listen to your teacher and answer.

英国在哪里？
英国人说英语吗？

中国在这里。
中国人说汉语。

中国在哪里？
中国人说英语吗？

英国在这里。
英国人说英语。

Song

🎧 **Listen and sing.**
05

 延伸活动：
学生唱歌曲前四句，老师唱后四句。老师在唱第五句时，随机指向一名学生，全班同学在老师唱完第六句时根据该学生情况回答前两句问题，如：他/她是 German。他/她说 German。（不会的单词可以用英文代替。）等老师唱完最后一句，再回答余下的两个问题，如：他/她会说汉语。他/她也会说英语。

Olá

Hola

Bonjour

Hallo

مرحبا

我是中国人，

我说汉语。

你是英国人，

你说英语。

他是哪国人？

他说什么语言？

他会不会说汉语？

他会不会说英语？

привет

Hello

你好

안녕하세요

こんにちは

课堂用语 Classroom language

错了。
Wrong.

为什么？
Why?

1 + 2 = ?

题目
Question

写一写 Write

1 Learn and trace the stroke. 老师示范笔画动作，学生跟着做：用手在空中画出"横折提"。

横折提

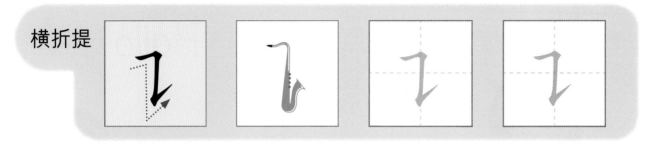

2 Learn the component. Trace 讠 to complete the characters.

说 语 话 谈

学生观察图片，提醒他们注意长颈鹿头顶的话框，引导他们发现言字旁字与说话、语言有关。

3 Circle the characters with 讠 and say their meanings.

悟

说
to speak

射

语
language

谢
to thank

悦

情

谁
who

准

请
please

"谁"字表示用语言询问对方的身份；"请"字的另一层意思是"邀请"，同样是用言语去请求他人。

4 Trace and write the character.

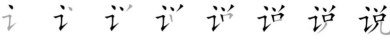

5 Write and say.

我会 说 英语。

我会 说 汉语。

汉字小常识 Did you know?

Colour the component that encloses another one red.
Colour the top-right component green.

Some characters include a component on all four sides. Other characters include a component that is placed on top and on the right.

国

回
红色

图
红色

可

句
绿色

式
绿色

多元学习 Connections

Cultures

外来词（loanword），又称外来语或借词，是一种语言从别的语言借来的词汇。汉语的外来词有音译和意译等形式。音译是直接按照原语言词汇的发音转换为汉语词汇，如"沙发（sofa）"。意译是根据意思来翻译，如"热狗（hot dog）"。

1 Languages influence each other. Learn about some loanwords in English and Chinese.

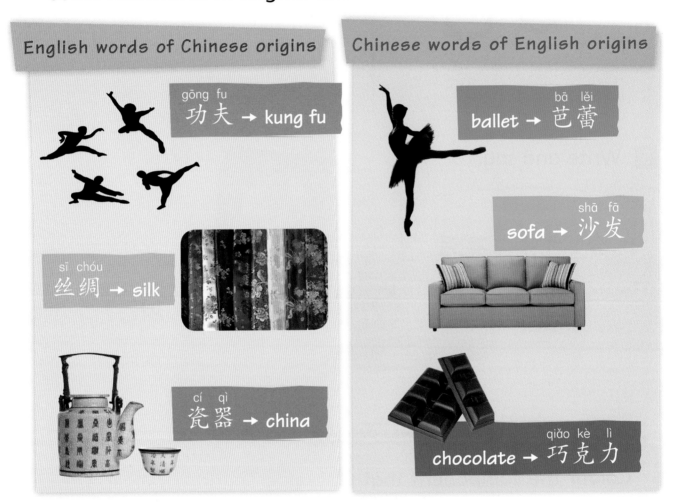

English words of Chinese origins

gōng fu
功夫 → kung fu

sī chóu
丝绸 → silk

cí qì
瓷器 → china

Chinese words of English origins

bā lěi
ballet → 芭蕾

shā fā
sofa → 沙发

qiǎo kè lì
chocolate → 巧克力

2 Practise the pronunciations of some more loanwords.

汉语 → 英语		英语 → 汉语	
tái fēng 台风 ↓ typhoon	lì zhī 荔枝 ↓ lychee	hamburger ↓ hàn bǎo bāo 汉堡包	bus ↓ bā shì 巴士

1 Match and write the letters. Say the names of the countries in Chinese after your teacher.

a Saudi Arabia   b China   c France   d Germany

e Portugal   f Russia   g Spain   h the United Kingdom

长城（the Great Wall）

中国 b

伊丽莎白塔／大本钟（the Elizabeth Tower/Big Ben）

英国 h

埃菲尔铁塔（the Eiffel Tower）

法国 c

凯旋门（the Brandenburg Gate）

德国 d

圣瓦西里大教堂（St. Basil's Cathedral）及周边

俄罗斯 f

发现者纪念碑（Monument to the Discoveries）

葡萄牙 e

奎尔公园（Park Güell）

西班牙 g

先知寺（the Prophet's Mosque）

沙特阿拉伯 a

2 Learn about world languages. In which languages can you greet your friend?

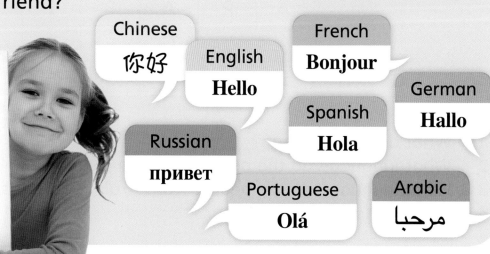

A world language is a language that is spoken internationally and is learnt and spoken by a large number of people as a second language.

Chinese
你好

English
Hello

French
Bonjour

German
Hallo

Spanish
Hola

Russian
привет

Portuguese
Olá

Arabic
مرحبا

温习 Checkpoint

1 Guess who they are. Write the letters and say in Chinese.

b a c

a 他不是英国人，他说英语。

b 她不是英国人，她说汉语，也会说英语。

c 她不是美国人，也不是中国人，她说英语。

提醒学生先通过分辨选项中的"他"和"她"来选出男孩 a，然后观察两个女孩。左边的女孩是亚洲人长相，而选项 b 中有关键信息"她说汉语"，则可初步判断该女孩是 b，再将选项 c 与右边的女孩对比，信息吻合，则该女孩是 c，左边的女孩确定是 b。

2 Complete the puzzle.

¹E	N	G	L	I	S	H			
	²S	P	A	N	I	S	H		
	F	R	E	N	C	H			
P	O	R	T	U	G	U	E	S	E
		R	U	S	S	I	A	N	
	³A	R	A	B	I	C			
	G	E	R	M	A	N			
⁴C	H	I	N	E	S	E			

1 What does 英语 mean?
2 What language do the people in Spain speak?
3 What language do the people from Arab countries speak?
4 What is 汉语 in English?

提醒学生做完题目后看看字谜中有多少种语言，以及这些语言和第19页的世界语言的关系。引导他们发现这些语言都是世界语言。

评核方法：

学生两人一组，互相考察评价表内单词和句子的听说读写。交际沟通部分由老师朗读要求，学生再互相对话。如果达到了某项技能要求，则用色笔将星星或小辣椒涂色。

3 Work with your friend. Colour the stars and the chilies.

Words	说	读	写
中国	☆	☆	🌶
中国人	☆	☆	🌶
英国	☆	☆	🌶
英国人	☆	☆	🌶
美国	☆	☆	🌶
美国人	☆	☆	🌶
汉语	☆	☆	🌶
英语	☆	☆	🌶
会	☆	☆	🌶
说	☆	☆	☆
写	☆	🌶	🌶
国家	☆	🌶	🌶

Words and sentences	说	读	写
你是哪国人？	☆	☆	🌶
我是中国人。	☆	☆	🌶
你会不会说英语？	☆	☆	🌶
我会说英语和汉语。	☆	☆	🌶

Talk about someone's nationality	☆
Talk about the languages someone speaks	☆

4 What does your teacher say?

My teacher says ...

评核建议：

根据学生课堂表现，分别给予"太棒了！(Excellent!)"、"不错！(Good!)"或"继续努力！(Work harder!)"的评价，再让学生圈出上方对应的表情，以记录自己的学习情况。

分享 Sharing

こんにちは

Words I remember

中国	zhōng guó	China
中国人	zhōng guó rén	Chinese (people)
英国	yīng guó	the United Kingdom
英国人	yīng guó rén	British
美国	měi guó	the United States
美国人	měi guó rén	American
汉语	hàn yǔ	Chinese (language)
英语	yīng yǔ	English (language)

Hallo

привет

延伸活动：
1　学生用手遮盖英文，读中文单词，并思考单词意思；
2　学生用手遮盖中文单词，看着英文说出对应的中文单词；
3　学生两人一组，尽量运用中文单词复述第4至9页内容。

Bonjour

你好

Hello

会	huì	can, to be able to
说	shuō	to speak
写	xiě	to write
国家	guó jiā	country

Other words

不同	bù tóng	not the same
都	dōu	all
一样	yī yàng	same
文字	wén zì	writing

Olá

OXFORD

UNIVERSITY PRESS

Oxford University Press is a department of the University of Oxford.
It furthers the University's objective of excellence in research, scholarship,
and education by publishing worldwide. Oxford is a registered trade mark of
Oxford University Press in the UK and in certain other countries

Published in Hong Kong by
Oxford University Press (China) Limited
39th Floor, One Kowloon, 1 Wang Yuen Street, Kowloon Bay,
Hong Kong

First Edition published in 2017

Illustrated by Anne Lee and Wildman

Photographs for reproduction permitted by Dreamstime.com

China National Publications Import & Export (Group) Corporation is an authorized distributor of
Oxford Elementary Chinese.

Please contact content@cnpiec.com.cn or 86-10-65856782

ISBN: 978-0-19-082196-8

10 9 8 7 6 5 4 3 2

Teacher's Edition
ISBN: 978-0-19-082208-8

10 9 8 7 6 5 4 3 2